RHYME CRAFT

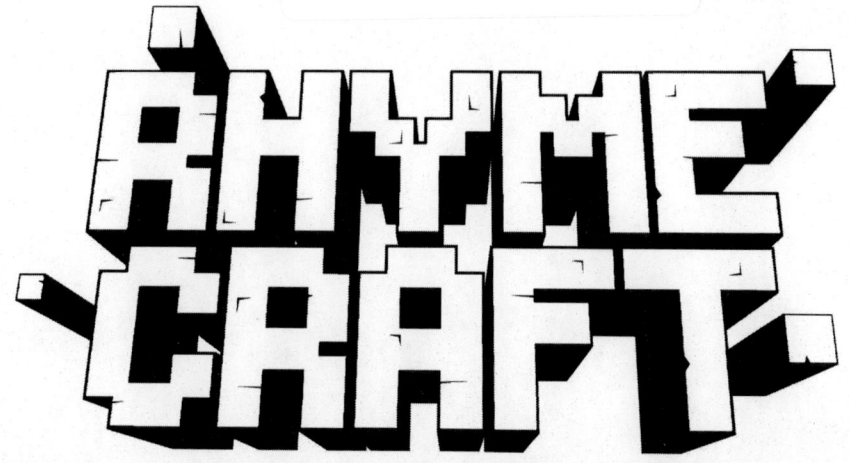

Welsh Poets

Edited By Donna Samworth

First published in Great Britain in 2018 by:

Young Writers
Remus House
Coltsfoot Drive
Peterborough
PE2 9BF
Telephone: 01733 890066
Website: www.youngwriters.co.uk

All Rights Reserved
Book Design by Ashley Janson
© Copyright Contributors 2018
SB ISBN 978-1-78896-543-9
Printed and bound in the UK by BookPrintingUK
Website: www.bookprintinguk.com
YB0362U

FOREWORD

Young Writers was established in 1991, dedicated to encouraging reading and creative writing in young people. Our nationwide writing initiatives are designed to inspire ideas and give pupils the incentive to write, and in turn develop literacy skills and confidence, whilst participating in a fun, imaginative activity.

Few things are more encouraging for the aspiring writer than seeing their own work in print, so we are proud that our anthologies are able to give young authors this unique sense of confidence and pride in their abilities.

For our latest competition, Rhymecraft, primary school pupils were asked to create a land in verse, using poetic techniques such as rhyme, simile and alliteration to bring their worlds to life. The result is an entertaining and imaginative anthology, filled to the brim with wonderful worlds and even a few nightmare lands too, so beware! Each poem showcases the creativity and talent of these budding new writers as they learn the skills of writing, and we hope you are as entertained by them as we are.

CONTENTS

Independent Entries

Dafydd Elis Jones (9)	1
Freya Rose Brunt (10)	2
Visakh Kartha (7)	4
Maci Elise Jones (11)	5
Ioan Morgan Hitchings (10)	6

Brackla Primary School, Brackla

Daisy Marie Williams (10)	7
Benjamin William Clark (10)	8
Molly Elizabeth Willsher (11)	10
Cleo Birt (11)	12
Aaron Hancox (10)	14
Aidan Williams (10)	16
Jack Beddow (10)	17
Emily Flower (11)	18
Jack Harvey (10)	19

Burry Port Community School, Burry Port

Erin Gravell (8)	20
Courtney Millington (9)	22
Ethan Naytor (10)	23
Jack Walters (9)	24
Finlay Stewart (9)	25
Brenden Williams (10)	26
Oliver Gregory Thomas (9)	27
Willow Freyja Badham-Evans (8)	28
Caleb Harmsworth (9)	29
Lowri Owens (10)	30
Cody Whatnall (7)	31
Emily Dallimore (8)	32
Leon Majaliwa (8)	33

Demi Jones (9)	34
Keith Webb (9)	35
Jake Stewart (7)	36
Eve Palfrey (9)	37
Shawri Freya Jones-Dennett (8)	38
Cody Etteridge (7)	39
Hayden Jaros-Grover (8)	40
Brooke Winter (9)	41
Ashley North (10)	42
Summer Marsh (10)	43
Lexi Gower (8)	44
Sión Davies (10)	45
Ryan Williams (9)	46
Kurtis Williams (10)	47
Evie O'Gorman (10)	48
Matthew Morgan (8)	49
Kian Mullins (10)	50
Nikkits Williams (9)	51
Liberty-Rose Jacob-McFarlane (8)	52
Harry Evans (8)	53
Lexi Ella Mae Howells (7)	54
Zack Morris (10)	55
Jamie Albrighton (7)	56
Ella Williams (10)	57
Logan Mogford (8)	58
Joe Fleming (8)	59
Ciara Fitzgerald (9)	60
Caitlin Clohessy (9)	61
Leon Albrightan (9)	62
Jamie Campbell (9)	63
Caiden Brown (7)	64
Verity Ann Taylor (8)	65
Reggie William Phillips (7)	66

Deighton Primary School, Tredegar

Alicia Charlotte Davies (11)	67
Megan Colling (10)	68
Evelyn Grace Pearsall (10)	69
Kelsey Morgan (11)	70
Ellie Colwell (11)	71
Millie Jones (11)	72
Tia Wetten (11)	73
Jasmine Wyatt (10)	74
Emma Havard (11)	75

High Street Primary School, Barry

Mia Lili Jennings (10)	76
Ruby D (9)	78
Eva Lilly Martin (10)	80
Ethan Williams (10)	82
Vidor Anderung (10)	83
Sophie Edwards (10)	84
Connor Ashill (10)	86
Sophie Dixon (8)	87
Joshua Perkins (8)	88
Sara Osman (8)	89
Wendy Lian (8)	90
Alexa Howells (7)	91
Griffin Enticott (7)	92
William Romans (7)	93
Savannah Abbott (8)	94
Ciaran-Jon Curnick (10)	95
Ellie May Stevens (10)	96
William Llewellyn Jones (9)	97

Palmerston Primary School, Barry

Kenny Logan Risby (9)	98
Isabelle Woodward (9)	99
Casey Moores (8)	100
Gethin John Conway (9)	101
Lilly Lane (9)	102
Shelby Oliver (8)	103
Skye Ford (9)	104

Pencoed Primary School, Pencoed

Beth Alicia Blank (11)	105
Layla Stevens (11)	106
Jack Anthony George (10)	108
Rhiannon Jade Witts (11)	110
Lucien Hope (7)	111
Ieuan Taylor (8)	112
Emrys James Curtis (8)	113
Ethan Twine (10)	114
Eve Frayne (11)	115
Fynnley David Farrow (8)	116
Rhiannon Woodfin (8)	117
Finn John Sewel (10)	118

Severn Primary School, Canton

Yaren Ince (8)	119
Isabel Drane (8)	120
Edward (7)	121
Ali Butt (8)	122
Bailey Shay Williams (7)	123
Millie Krebs-Jachimiak (7)	124
Taha Ibrahim (7)	125

St Andrew's Primary School, Newport

Layla Gabica (10)	126
Kayley Haynes (11)	128
Sarah Curticean (11)	129
Shakyah Powell (10)	130

St Helen's Primary School, Swansea

Khadiza Ali (11)	131
Tahmina Uddin (10)	132
Akram Ali (10)	134
Nafisha Parvin (11)	136
Saamira Karim (11)	137
Alisha Ali (10)	138
Amina Khatun (10)	139
Ali Utub (10)	140

Sara Nour (10)	141
Saabira Karim (11)	142
Tanzina Begum (11)	143
Elena Velichkova (10)	144
Riya Rahman (10)	145

Ysgol Gynradd Gymraeg Caerffili, Caerphilly

Megan Rhys Godfrey (9)	146
Sophie Jackson (9)	148
Meleri Ann Godfrey (9)	149
Isabella Ewings (11)	150
Alice Elizabeth Todd (10)	151
Heulwen Crimmins (9)	152

Ysgol Nantgaredig, Nantgaredig

Ioan Jones (8)	153
Grace Hobbs Rees (7)	154
Carys Thomas (7)	155
Honor Kernahan (8)	156
Nancie Gooding (7)	157
Betsan Quick (8)	158

Ysgol Trewen, Beulah

Eluned Meredith Morgan (10)	159
Kelsey Carter (8)	160

Ysgol Y Ddwylan, Newcastle Emlyn

Gwen Sandra Samantha Nichols-Long (11)	161
Lili Pocsai (10)	162
Ianto Lloyd (9)	165
Nyle Berry (10)	166
Liam Evans (10)	168
Eirinn Amy O'Neill (9)	170
Daniel Hulston (8)	171
Lacey (10) & Madison Hands	172
Evie Haf Denton (8)	173
Halle Mai Evans (10)	174
Alis Bevan (8)	175

Jack Dentten (10)	176
Amelie Gardner (10)	177
Olivia Thompson Brook (8)	178
Lola Thomas (10)	179
Rhys Geraint Ridley-Bloom (9)	180
Katie Ann Jones (10)	181
Lily Lamb (10)	182
Crwys Daniel (9)	183
Tyler Dowling (8)	184
Finley Stephens (9)	185
Callum Long (9)	186
Amber Aryana Varrow (8)	187
Loren Gwenllian Jones (8)	188
Katie Hunt (9)	189
Dafydd Nichols-Evans (9)	190
Rafia Alam (7)	191
Charlie Fillmore (9)	192
Layla Dowling (9)	193
Spencer Sando Varrow (8)	194
Chloe Hatch (10)	195
Julia Strzemkowska (10)	196
Connor Dion Humphreys (9)	197
Mia Fulstow (10)	198
Sara Davies (8)	199
Marley Bussey (8)	200
Iestyn Kedward-Jones (10)	201
Ivy Thomas (8)	202
Scarlett Poppy James (8)	203

Ystruth Primary School, East Pentwyn

Lainie Curtis (10)	204
Olivia May Martyn (10)	205
Rhys John Selwood (10)	206
Mia Hoskins (11)	207
Grace Tandy (10)	208
Leah James (11)	209
Jessica Ann Griffiths (11)	210
Troy Shaun Thomas (10)	211
Grace Gwillym (10)	212
Jack Williams (11)	213
Tayah Foulkes (11)	214
Ruby-Mae Perkins (10)	215

Logan Carter (10) 216
Grace Norris (10) 217

THE POEMS

Gaming Wonderland

I travel to my world of gaming
Away from my mum's complaining,
Where everything is a marvellous wonderland,
Positioned upon my TV stand.

I can choose to be anyone with this console,
Super Mario jumping down a hole
To Sonic zooming past a spiky mole,
Or completing Zelda, my ultimate goal.

My favourite without a doubt is my Xbox,
Building anything with virtual blocks.
My mum reminds me of the time on the clock,
Yelling, "Dafydd put away your socks!"

I also like my dad's iPad,
Playing this never makes me sad,
Hours of fun are always had,
That is until my mum gets really mad!

Dafydd Elis Jones (9)

Yummyland

My house is made of gingerbread,
And a chocolate biscuit is my bed.
My garden path has no bumps,
It is made of marshmallow Flumps.

Strawberry milk makes up the lake,
With a bendy bridge of chocolate Flake,
There are lots and lots of gummy bears,
Sitting on the liquorice chairs.

There's a Skittle rainbow in the sky,
With candyfloss clouds floating by.
It does not rain wet raindrops,
But lots of coloured lollipops.

My world is such a magical place,
Where unicorns are commonplace.
The fairy castle is a must,
Made with lots of pixie dust.

Everything is edible,
Which makes your tummy always full.

Come and visit if you like,
And sample some of these delights.

Freya Rose Brunt (10)

The Earth

I can hear children laughing and playing,
I can see birds flying all around,
I can smell fresh air,
I can taste seasalt at the seaside,
I can touch shells at the beach.

I can hear birds tweeting,
I can see cars driving past,
I can smell roses in the garden,
I can touch animals.

I can hear waves crashing,
I can see planes flying in the air,
I can smell food cooking,
I can taste car fumes,
I can touch the bark on the trees,
Earth is my lovely home.

Visakh Kartha (7)

Cloud 9

I am going to Cloud 9,
Everything is going to shine,
The weather is fine,
And the candy is divine,
Look at that unicorn,
Isn't it pretty?
It's all so glittery.
Sparkly and shimmery,
There's nothing dull,
It's so full,
For where will this paradise take me?
Who will know?

Maci Elise Jones (11)

Welsh Rugby

W ales are the best at rugby
A gainst their opponents of old.
L ineouts, scrums, rucks and mauls
E ngland, France, Ireland, Italy and Scotland
S tand no chance at all. Wales will win the Six Nations!

Ioan Morgan Hitchings (10)

Sweet City

Lollipop flowers, sticky but sweet
Chocolate mice and jelly spiders scurry around my feet
Sweets, candy and sugar galore
All the goodies I adore.

Little girls play with gummy bear toys
But not with jelly worms, they're just for boys
The pink, fluffy clouds are made of candyfloss
A bright blue sky they steal across.

The crunchy cone squirts out ice cream
Making the gingerbread children beam
As the melted chocolate river runs
People sail along on hot cross buns.

The forest is made of candy cane trees
That sway side to side in the hush of the breeze
My candy land is a magical place
A place where you can stuff your face.

Daisy Marie Williams (10)
Brackla Primary School, Brackla

Seasons

Spring
In the spring, daffodils grow,
All the snow has to go,
All the fields will turn greener,
Flowers and plants will appear.

Summer
All the days will get longer,
The sun will shine much hotter,
Water sparkles in the sun,
Time to go outside for some fun.

Autumn
In the autumn, leaves turn brown
Then the leaves will fall down,
All the trees will look bare,
All the plants will not be there.

Winter
In the winter comes the chills,
When we pay more for our heating bills,
When it's raining, we stay inside,
Keeping from the cold outside.

Without seasons, there will be no change,
Seasons keep us entertained,
What about the autumn fall,
Or about the summer's warmth,
We love seasons, we love change
We'll always be happy every day.

Benjamin William Clark (10)
Brackla Primary School, Brackla

A World Of Seasons

I know a place,
Far, far away in space,
That is divided by seasons,
You should go there, here is a number of reasons:

Spring
Spring is a large meadow,
That is especially beautiful when fireflies glow,
It is full of new life,
And empty of strife.

Summer
A cool wind comes through the warm air,
And runs like fingers through your hair
As you watch the sunset,
After a day of messing round and getting wet.

Autumn
It may be cold but you can get cosy,
Watching the fire with your cheeks rosy,
As you get ready to play bingo,
Leaves fall outside your window.

Winter
The ice glistens,
And you can hear sleigh bells if you listen,
Everybody's Christmas shopping,
Little do they know, the festive season's never stopping!

Molly Elizabeth Willsher (11)
Brackla Primary School, Brackla

Why War?

Why must I leave my love so soon?
I feel I haven't said goodbye
It's like I'm trapped inside my head
Watching the days go by.

I see my gun flashing
Tears splashing
Cannons booming
Soldiers fuming.

Why must life end so quickly?
It's like I was born yesterday
This war has gone so slowly
Half of us are going astray.

I see my gun flashing
Tears splashing
Cannons booming
Soldiers fuming.

Why must we have this stupid war?
Our lives are all at risk

If only there was another way
Instead of using an iron fist.

I see my gun flashing
Blood splashing
Cannons booming
Soldiers fuming.

I hear the gunfire trailing off
An airstrike overhead
They whistle through the bombing run
Now everyone is dead!

Cleo Birt (11)
Brackla Primary School, Brackla

My Star Wars Land

I have a Star Wars land,
I know it like the back of my hand,
There's deserts and forests and mountains to climb,
And the great Han Solo earning a dime.

My favourite planet is Endor,
Where the wild, savage Ewoks dance in splendor,
There are green blocks for the grass,
And blue for the sky,
There's purple for the sea,
But I don't know why.

There is more than one planet,
Some are cold, some are hot,
Some are cubes, some are not,
The spaceships are blocks,
And flat on the side,
They zoom through space.

I enjoy the ride,
The people and beasts look different to home,

All have square heads,
Never a dome.

So that is my galaxy far, far away
Where Minecraft meets Star Wars,
A place we can play.

Aaron Hancox (10)
Brackla Primary School, Brackla

Marshmallow Meadows

As I walk down Marshmallow Meadows,
Past fields of luscious liquorice lumps
Springing on a pathway of pillows,
Soft as cotton, no lumps or bumps.

In the distance, the sound of splashing,
Of a swirling chocolate river
Jelly babies are relaxing,
Rowing boats, hither and thither.

Above, biscuit birds swooping swiftly,
Through the sparkling, cloudless skies
Coloured gummy bears waddle slowly,
Towards me, laughter in their eyes.

As I leave Marshmallow Meadows
A repetitive noise wakes me from my slumber.

Aidan Williams (10)
Brackla Primary School, Brackla

World Of Black

Black is the smoke, circling the trees
Black are the stripes of the bumblebees
At the sight of the colour black, I beam
Black is the colour of which I dream.

Black is the night sky, still and dark
Black is the noticeboard at the park
At the mention of the colour black, I beam
Black is the colour of which I dream.

Black is the tar; way, way down
Black is the colour of a witch's gown
At the absence of the colour black, I beam
Black is the colour of which I dream.

Jack Beddow (10)
Brackla Primary School, Brackla

The Senseless World

I can hear monsters that we would only imagine
Moaning, groaning, slowly wasting away
I can feel their icy breath making a sudden chill
Run down my spine as they near
I can see raging fires that have been used
As torches to guide the horrible beast's way
I can smell the rotting, decaying land
Dying all around
I can almost taste the toxic, foul air
That makes my eyes water and my stomach turn.

Emily Flower (11)
Brackla Primary School, Brackla

Candy Land

The rain dropped just like honey,
The ground fluffy and puffy,
As pink as candyfloss
The candy, cracking canes are hard
Just like bark on a tree,
The sky is see-through
Just like a giant pink lollipop
Also, the water is hot chocolate
Flowing from a waterfall,
Clouds are like white candyfloss,
The waves are crispy just like crisps,
There is no harm in the world of candy.

Jack Harvey (10)
Brackla Primary School, Brackla

Glitter City

In Glitter City, everything is so pretty,
The stars twinkle so bright at night,
It's such a beautiful sight!
But, shhh, let me tell you, there is a secret to be told
So, please listen carefully, let the story unfold...
Glitter City has not always been as above,
And it all began with a sweet flying dove
The dove was cursed by a wicked old witch,
Who wanted the dove to be her snitch
But when the dove refused, her heart was bruised
She became very angry and with a whoosh of her wand,
She made it rain which drove everyone insane
It rained for days which got the people down,
And after months of rain, they wore nothing but a frown
The light had gone and everything was dark,
But then one morning I woke with a start
I opened my curtains with a thump in my heart

I crept down the stairs being very cautious
Blinking my eyes I felt very nauseous
For something amazing had happened that night
All of the dark had turned to light
The curse had gone, everyone cheered and in a flitter
There was glitter!
It poured from the clouds and covered the city
And that's how it became so very pretty!

Erin Gravell (8)
Burry Port Community School, Burry Port

Candy Land

Here in Candy Land, all is tasty and sweet
But no sweet rain or snow
We use candy wrapper bows
And nothing but candy lives in Candy Land.
We love candy here but no more
Ice cream houses, it melts
Skittles are too small
Cookies on all the roofs with gummy dummies
All is sweet here in Candy Land
Everyone likes it here
Gummy bear pets live there
But here's a story you should know
Candy Land has never ever been this peaceful
Since the war started down the road
Candy King turkey was eaten
But if you believe, you may find
Candy Land around the corner.

Courtney Millington (9)
Burry Port Community School, Burry Port

Candy Land

Everything in this land is sweet and neat
There's Skittles everywhere which you can eat
Come and stuff your face and fill yourself with grace
But never take King Candy's sweets or he'll put you between his enormous, smelly feet!
The lollipop trees are really lovely but watch out for the honeybees
The houses are made of caramel bricks and they even have a chimney made of Twix
The fields are made of candy corn, but watch out for the cola thorns
So come on down to Candy Land and you'll feel like you're singing for a huge brass band!

Ethan Naytor (10)
Burry Port Community School, Burry Port

Crazy Land

Welcome to Crazy Land
A bright and colourful city
Where the animals are friendly
And everyone is pretty
The sea is as clear as a pane of glass
Life is so wonderful here
You don't want the time to pass
Flowers bloom all year round
They grow everywhere
Not just the ground
Children play all day long
Laughing, joking and singing songs
Parents don't work
They play too
They don't live in houses
They live in the zoo
So come to Crazy Land
You will arrive normal
But you will leave crazy.

Jack Walters (9)
Burry Port Community School, Burry Port

Candy Land

C andyfloss clouds raining sweet
A n apple is crunchy but so are sweets
N utella is delicious, also great on pancakes
D elicious, warm waffles covered in Nutella
Y ellow, green, red and blue Skittles.

C andy cane and lolly trees, very yummy
A pple sours make you think you're going to explode
N utella ponds covered in marshmallows, candy houses on top
E verything as colourful as Skittles
S ome ponds are as clear as glass, very nice with the grass.

Finlay Stewart (9)
Burry Port Community School, Burry Port

The Land Of Cakes

I'd like to live in the Land of Cakes,
Although the houses may take a long time to bake.
They'd be worth the wait, all made to each owner's taste,
Chocolate, strawberry and vanilla
No need for haste, there'd be no waste,
Flat, bungalow, house or villa
All would taste delicious in my Land of Cakes.

The rain would fall as cream,
The snow as marshmallows,
Where children would never scream,
Children would bounce off rainbows
And always have sweet, sweet dreams
In my Land of Cakes.

Brenden Williams (10)
Burry Port Community School, Burry Port

Trampoline City

In my city, there are no cars,
No bikes, no trains, no aeroplanes!
We bounce, we jump, we somersault,
To get from A to B,
There are no roads or pavements,
It's just our trampolines.

We bounce and bounce like jumping beans,
But it's always fun when we do it in teams,
Flying through the fresh morning air
Bouncing, enjoying without a care.

Come and visit Trampoline City,
See the sights, the highs and the lows are so pretty.

Welcome, welcome to Trampoline City!

Oliver Gregory Thomas (9)
Burry Port Community School, Burry Port

Unicorn Land

Unicorn Land is the place to go
Follow me through the magical door
The best time to go is in the night
When they gather together under the moonlight.

You should see them all standing there
Glittery horns and long rainbow hair
My favourite unicorn is called Mandy
She smells delicious just like candy.

Unicorn land is bold and bright
Full of colour, a beautiful sight
Rivers made of chocolate ice cream
Come and see for yourself.

It's like a dream.

Willow Freyja Badham-Evans (8)
Burry Port Community School, Burry Port

Historical Land

H istory is no longer history
I cannot believe my eyes
S axons fighting Vikings
T udors beheading enemies
O bama becoming president
R omans ruling strictly
I nventions by Victorians
C romwell banning parties
A rmstrong walking on the moon
L lama farming by Incas.

L incoln ending slavery
A lbert and Queen Victoria
N asty Great Fire of London
D o not ever forget this land!

Caleb Harmsworth (9)
Burry Port Community School, Burry Port

Unicandy Land!

In Unicandy Land, everything is grand
Unimonkeys swing from strawberry laces,
In the Fruitella forest, of all places.
Unicorns prancing on the Double Decker dance floor
There is no stopping them now, they're dancing galore!
Chocolate rivers are where gummy snakes slither
Flying pigs leap across candyfloss clouds
They won the candyfloss race
They received lots of bows
So if you like candy, come visit this place
It is where you can stuff your face!

Lowri Owens (10)
Burry Port Community School, Burry Port

Dinosaur Land

In Dinosaur Land, the dinosaurs rule
Trust me, they are very cool
Some have big sharp teeth and are quite scary
Others are enormous and all hairy
Some have long necks and eat trees, they just walk past
But watch out for the ones that eat people, quick run fast
It's a magical land, close your eyes and see
Let's take a trip, you and me
Picture them all there, walking free
Can you see some flying? It's amazing, don't you agree?

Cody Whatnall (7)
Burry Port Community School, Burry Port

Dolphin Land

Dolphin Land is big and grand
Dolphin Land is near the sand
Dolphin Land is in the sea
Dolphin Land is fun for me.

Dolphin Land has lots of groups
For me to chase right through the hoops
There's lots of places to take a peek
When we are playing hide-and-seek.

There's lots of tunnels with some bends
For me to play in with my friends
So come and join us, take my hand
Come and play in Dolphin Land.

Emily Dallimore (8)
Burry Port Community School, Burry Port

Chocolate Land

I give my chocolate a shake,
And laugh until my belly aches
The only other sounds that break
Are of distant waves and birds that wake.

The chocolate land is mighty warm and deep
And I have many promises to keep
After cake and lots of sleep
Sweet dreams tickle my feet.

I rise from my gentle bed
With thoughts of chocolate in my head
I eat Nutella with lots of bread
Ready for the day ahead.

Leon Majaliwa (8)
Burry Port Community School, Burry Port

Candy Land

In Candy Land,
The sweets are grand
Flowers made of cotton candy
That come in very handy.

Trees made from jelly beans
Filled with our dreams,
Streams filled with Skittles
For me to have a little nibble.

Rainbow colours,
Like no others,
Spreading happiness all around.

It's a beautiful place,
As the look on my face,
I will save you a place,
Because I am ace.

Demi Jones (9)
Burry Port Community School, Burry Port

Candy Land

Welcome to Candy Land,
Where everything is full of sherbet sand
Chocolate monkeys swinging from strawberry laces
Liquorice snakes slithering through chocolate ponds.

People stuffing their mouths with loads of sweets
You can find hundreds of treats
Everybody's looking shocked at what they can find in the shops.

Raining Skittles in the air
But one of them tastes like a juicy pear.

Keith Webb (9)
Burry Port Community School, Burry Port

Candy Land

Candy Land,
This land is made of candy
Everything is edible if you want to eat
Grab some if you want to eat a treat
It might look delicious but it might not be nutritious
It might look yummy but the trees might be a bit too gummy
Some have a ride on the candy cane train but it might be insane
Try some ice cream but it might make you scream
Try some Starburst but it might make your brain burst.

Jake Stewart (7)
Burry Port Community School, Burry Port

Candy Land

Candy Land is the best in the world,
It is sweet, cool, fun and extremely swirled.

With new things happening every day
Like the sweet and swirly river
Will no doubt give a shiver
It's exciting and enticing
With tonnes and tonnes of icing.

Sweet and sour Candy Land
Is fun, sticky and very funny
With lollipop people running around
While the toxic waste cools down.

Eve Palfrey (9)
Burry Port Community School, Burry Port

Candy Village

Up in the mountains, there's streams of sweets,
Trees and valleys filled with treats,
Everywhere you go there are always things to eat,
With lots of lovely people to meet.

Candy Village is full of unicorns
With sparkle and glitter,
That makes the candy sweet, sour and bitter
Every day in Candy Village, it's fun, fun, fun
When you're filling up your tum, tum, tum.

Shawri Freya Jones-Dennett (8)
Burry Port Community School, Burry Port

My Birthday Party

My birthday party is today,
It's time to play.
Opening my toys,
I'm really hoping for a Gameboy.

My friends have arrived,
It's time to go outside.
Waiting for my clown,
This party is the talk of the town.

Everyone has now gone,
My house looks like it's been hit by a bomb.
My party was amazing,
But it's my mum that needs praising.

Cody Etteridge (7)
Burry Port Community School, Burry Port

The Football Stadium

The stadium walls are really high, they almost go up to the sky,

There's so many supporters in the crowd, all cheering and shouting really loud,

The football kit is bright and white but after the game, it's sweaty and wet,

The game goes without a hitch, playing on the football pitch,

Yes! My team has won, now let's celebrate and have some fun.

Hayden Jaros-Grover (8)
Burry Port Community School, Burry Port

Unicorn Life

The tiger and the unicorn were fighting for the crown
The tiger chased the unicorn all around about the town
Some gave them white bread and some gave them brown,
Some gave them cheesecake and drummed them out of time
Then the tiger and unicorn stopped fighting for the crown,
They started to hang round together in town
The tiger and the unicorn ended up best friends.

Brooke Winter (9)
Burry Port Community School, Burry Port

Everyday Life In School

S chool is for learning, everyone knows
C aring and sharing
H elping each other along the way
O ver the year, new friends you will meet
O ne of your lessons will seem the best
L istening intently to pupils' lives

But mainly teachers that you think are the best
School is as fun as can be.

Ashley North (10)
Burry Port Community School, Burry Port

Magic Unicorns Are Amazing

Unicorns are fluffy
Unicorns are sweet
Unicorns are magical
Unicorns are cute.

Unicorns live in a forest
Magical river flowing through
The magical tree
The sun is bright as a light.

Unicorns play with magic
Unicorns fly high as a kite
Unicorns dance as a rainbow
Unicorns play with other unicorns.

Summer Marsh (10)
Burry Port Community School, Burry Port

Candy Land

Candy Land is different to what we see every day
I hear the lemon drop rain splash against the chocolate mud
I see lollipop trees swaying in the breeze
I smell the peppermint mist coming from the candy cane forest
I taste fresh gingerbread men
I touch soft sherbet sand and lime-green seaweed.

I love Candy Land, it's great.

Lexi Gower (8)
Burry Port Community School, Burry Port

Fish Land

The sea smells of old, stinky socks
Fish bashing into rocks
There are tiny fish and fat fish that love to eat
But coming their way is a sea creature
That is as colossal as a cruise ship...
A great white shark with sabre teeth
Sparkling skin, he snapped and and snipped
Fish danced until the sun set as the huge shark surrendered.

Sión Davies (10)
Burry Port Community School, Burry Port

Biscuits Land

Biscuits are my favourite treat, three in my hand, ready to eat.
Houses made of cookie dough, bonded together with jam, you know,
Jammie Dodger flowers with special sweet powers,
A coconut ring for the marriage of the king
They'll seal their vows with a Party Ring
This would be my favourite land, with three biscuits in each hand.

Ryan Williams (9)
Burry Port Community School, Burry Port

Birthday Land

B est day of the year
I t's all about you
R eady for fun and games
T reats, sweets and all you can eat
H ave a great time all day long
D rape banners and balloons all over the house
A nd lots of gifts for you to enjoy
Y ou will love Birthday Land, sounds great to me!

Kurtis Williams (10)
Burry Port Community School, Burry Port

Candy World

Come and visit Candy World
Where everything is sweet
You can stuff your faces with chocolate and sweets
There are carrots full of jelly beans
Chocolate bunnies burying chocolate cream
Candyfloss clouds covering the light
Melted chocolate on top of marshmallow
Is imagination all we need?

Evie O'Gorman (10)
Burry Port Community School, Burry Port

Under The Pirate Ship

What lurks under a pirate ship?
A shipwreck filled with gold.

A huge blue whale with a great big tail
Squirting water wherever he goes.

A submarine being chased by a shark
Who is hungry for his tea!

So watch out on the pirate ship,
For what lurks beneath the sea!

Matthew Morgan (8)
Burry Port Community School, Burry Port

Candyland

Candy canes everywhere
Minty freshness in the air.

Ice cream raining from the sky
Just as tasty as apple pie.

Marshmallow trampolines covered in jelly beans
Chocolate fountains, gumdrop mountains.

Sherbet sand in my hand,
Oh, what a wonderful land!

Kian Mullins (10)
Burry Port Community School, Burry Port

Snow And Ice

S now is pretty and my land is snowy
N o school on Monday or Tuesday
O n the day that the snow fell
W ow, we made a mini and a big snowman.

I ce was cold
C reate snowmen in the cold snow
E at the snow, it is so much fun.

Nikkits Williams (9)
Burry Port Community School, Burry Port

Unicorn

Unicorn, unicorn, unicorn
How beautiful you are to see
Unicorn, unicorn, unicorn,
You're as white as snow can be.

Unicorn, unicorn, unicorn,
You're mystical and enchanting
That's what I see
Unicorn, unicorn, unicorn
A magical friend to me.

Liberty-Rose Jacob-McFarlane (8)
Burry Port Community School, Burry Port

Food City

Not far away, around the corner, is Food City
Where things smell good and look so pretty
The food so tasty
From pies to pasties even the pastry,
Fruit and vegetables, even some meat
Not forgetting something sweet
Yummy, yummy in my tummy
Delicious food.

Harry Evans (8)
Burry Port Community School, Burry Port

Candy Town

In Candy Town, it rains delicious candy
You live in a cool candy house
There is a nice candy rainbow there
There are yummy candy canes and lollipops you can eat,
You can also eat the grass that is made out of strawberry laces
It is fun in Candy Town, come visit.

Lexi Ella Mae Howells (7)
Burry Port Community School, Burry Port

Holidays

H appy and excited
O ff we go
L aughing on the mammoth beach
I ce cream is the best
D iscos, shows and late nights
A ll-you-can-eat buffet
Y ellow, golden sun
S wimming the day away as fast as lightning.

Zack Morris (10)
Burry Port Community School, Burry Port

Candy Land

I want rainbows in the sky
Unicorns flying by,
Chocolate rivers flooding by,
Candy buildings to taste and try.

Pink, fluffy candyfloss ground,
Gingerbread men all around,
Music playing a happy sound,
This is where I will be found.

Jamie Albrighton (7)
Burry Port Community School, Burry Port

The Sweet Forest!

In the forests, chocolate rivers run,
On the ground, here they come
Chocolate rivers flow like there's no tomorrow
Candy canes are everywhere, blowing on the trees from the air
The clouds are like candyfloss
When you eat it, they move across.

Ella Williams (10)
Burry Port Community School, Burry Port

Football

F riends come to play
O utside every day
O ver in the fields
T o kick a ball about
B efore it gets too late,
A game must be won
L osing's not an option
L iverpool are number one.

Logan Mogford (8)
Burry Port Community School, Burry Port

Gaming Land

G aming Land is where you play video games all day
A nd no toilet breaks
M inecraft, Mario Kart, PlayStation and more
I maginations run wild
N o school
G aming all day long, life will never change.

Joe Fleming (8)
Burry Port Community School, Burry Port

Cookie Land

Cookies are everywhere, falling from the sky,
From way up in the air, the people in Cookie Land all say hi
The people in Cookie Land throw cookies in the air for celebration
Occasions for you and me
So join in and have some fun with me.

Ciara Fitzgerald (9)
Burry Port Community School, Burry Port

Biscuit Land

Biscuit Land is really sweet
Custard creams under your feet
If you go there, you might meet
A biscuit horse, it's such a treat
Jammie Dodger trees by a chocolate stream
Oh what fun is life, it's like I am in a dream!

Caitlin Clohessy (9)
Burry Port Community School, Burry Port

Parkour

I love parkour,
It gets me out the door,
No rivers, teams or points for me,
I am as happy as can be.

I jump and climb,
Leaving the streets behind,
Moving past obstacles in my way
A new trick every day.

Leon Albrightan (9)
Burry Port Community School, Burry Port

Favourite Game Land

F ighting for the win
O ther people fighting
R unning everywhere
T rying to win
N ever giving up
I try so hard
T o get the win
E veryone has done well.

Jamie Campbell (9)
Burry Port Community School, Burry Port

Spooky Land

My land is a spooky land
It's very scary and
Some things are even hairy
Some things bite and
Some things will give you a fright!
So be very careful and stay there,
It's not a very nice place.

Caiden Brown (7)
Burry Port Community School, Burry Port

Candy Village

C andy Village is a sweet place to be
A nd the village homes are cupcakes
N ot a bit of stone
D andelions are just jelly babies
Y ou can come for a sweet treat.

Verity Ann Taylor (8)
Burry Port Community School, Burry Port

Land Of The Old

A diplodocus was a mighty old beast
He roamed and he groaned
While he ate all the leaves
Then sat by a rock
Which looked like a hat.

Reggie William Phillips (7)
Burry Port Community School, Burry Port

Colourful Land

C andy swimming across the chocolate
O bbys for the kids to play on
L ook inside the gingerbread castle, the kings are candy canes
O ut in Sprinkle Snow, the kids making snowflakes
U nicorns resting on the fluffy clouds
R ainucorns trying to bite the clouds
F unny clowns zooming down in their little cars
U nicorns flying peacefully off their clouds
L ike ICT people showing them how to play games.

Alicia Charlotte Davies (11)
Deighton Primary School, Tredegar

Candy Land

In Candy Land, the sweets are grand
It all tastes so good so you understood
There's a chocolate river so you can slither
The leaves are mean and full of cream
It's all so pretty, what a city
It's full of Skittles, so you can whistle
It's full of pops so you can pop
And it's all so sweet so you can beat
It's all so yummy, full of gummies
So thank you for visiting at Candy Land.

Megan Colling (10)
Deighton Primary School, Tredegar

Sugar Dreams

S ugar dreams I used to have
U nicorns I used to follow
G umdrops I used to lick
A chocolate lake I used to swim in
R ose-red candy canes I used to eat.

D reams full of sugar
R ainbows I used to climb
E ven though I am older now, my
A dventures will always stay
M ore adventures in every dream
S ugar dreams.

Evelyn Grace Pearsall (10)
Deighton Primary School, Tredegar

JoJo Bows

Bows, bows, I love them all,
Yellow, green and indigo
There are so many colours, like green and blue,
I wish I could have them all for me and you,
Yo yo, it is JoJo,
I have an amazing dog called Bow-Bow!
Every bow is unique,
You will never find the same bow in another
Bow-tique
You can find bright bows and light,
You can even find bows that you wear all night!

Kelsey Morgan (11)
Deighton Primary School, Tredegar

Candy Land

In Candy Land, it all tastes nice
Because there is no such thing as spice,
Everything tastes sweet,
There is sure to be no meat.

All the trees blow
Fireflies dance as they glow
Things are attached with honey,
There are trillions of money.

The sour we hate,
Chocolate is great,
This place is enchanted,
Come and get your wishes granted!

Ellie Colwell (11)
Deighton Primary School, Tredegar

Magic Land

In Magic Land, the clouds are alive
And cats can drive
It's never dark! Always bright
Even when it's night
There are loads of lollipops
Lots of maple syrup drops
Constant music
Did I mention the candyfloss clouds, the sky's silk
The world's so colourful
Everyone's cheerful
It's Magic Land
Oh no, grand!

Millie Jones (11)
Deighton Primary School, Tredegar

Blue Colour

Blue is the colour,
Football is the game,
We're all together,
And winning is our aim,
So cheer all up through the sun and rain
'Cause Chelsea, Chelsea is our name!

Chelsea is our name,
We win every game,
Even if it's rain,
We will feel no pain,
We are Chelsea!

Tia Wetten (11)
Deighton Primary School, Tredegar

Sweet Land

S weeties are the best for everyone
W ishing, wishing for the sweets, more delicious
E ating lovely delicious sweets,
E njoying the taste of the super sour sweets
T asting the coldness of the candy canes,
S leeping under the sweet angels in the sky.

Jasmine Wyatt (10)
Deighton Primary School, Tredegar

Barbie Land

B right and colourful home
A bility to be in Barbie Land
R olling green hills in the countryside
B eautiful Barbie in the streets
I magination
E veryone's friends.

Emma Havard (11)
Deighton Primary School, Tredegar

Underwater Land Poem

I dove down deep into the sea
The fish dove and swam with me,
I gripped my torch in my hand
And shone it at an underwater land.

There was a beautiful pearl castle,
And a mermaid with earrings of tassels,
She grabbed me by the hand and pulled me around,
Then she let me stand on the sandy ground.

She gave me a kiss then she swam off,
Then I heard a sudden cough,
I looked around and there was nothing there,
I thought and scratched my hair.

Then a fish came out of the blue,
I had no idea what to do!
He wagged his little tail,
There was a gigantic whale!

The enormous whale,
(Whose name was Dale)

Spoke in a deep, deep voice and said:
"Don't mind the little fish, his name is Fred!"

We swam for a while,
Then... Oh no, a crocodile!
We swam so fast I couldn't see
The crocodile who was behind me!

I hid behind a rock
Then I climbed onto the clock,
Now it was time to go to sleep for the night,
I held my teddy really tight.

Mia Lili Jennings (10)
High Street Primary School, Barry

Underwater Land Poem

I dove down deep into the sea
The fish dove and swam with me,
I gripped my torch in my hand
And shone it at an underwater land.

I saw lots of shells on the ground,
Come and have a look at what I found
I saw a glimpse of something shiny…
Was it big or was it tiny?

I tightly gripped my torch in my hand,
And swam in a cave that was not very grand,
There was coral all over the ground
And a fish that made such a beautiful sound.

I swam in a shady, wrecked shipwreck
And bumped the back of my neck
I touched something in the sand
I picked it up and it was a toy hand.

I saw an octopus with lots of legs
And then I saw a mummy fish laying eggs

There was a jellyfish that I named Jerry
And I figured he liked to eat blueberries.

A fish swam up to me
And very gently nudged my knee...

Ruby D (9)
High Street Primary School, Barry

Underwater Land Poem

I dove down deep into the sea
The fish dove and swam with me,
I gripped my torch in my hand
And shone it at an underwater land.

What I could see was a surprise for me,
There was glistening coral as far as I could see,
There was not much commotion,
At the bottom of the ocean.

I swam along some more,
And more and more was what I saw
I saw a baby shark,
In an underwater park.

I saw a family of fish,
Who were moving with a bit of swish,
I saw a big whale,
With a ginormous blue tail.

In the distance, there was a cave,
And the sharks were using fish as their slaves,

Voices were becoming clear,
As the end of my time was near.

I hope to visit again soon,
In this wonderful blue lagoon,
As I reach the surface of the sea,
My friends wave hi to me.

Eva Lilly Martin (10)
High Street Primary School, Barry

Underwater Land Poem

I dove down deep into the sea,
The fish dove and swam with me,
I gripped my torch in my hand
And shone it at an underwater land.

As I swam lower down,
I moved closer without a frown,
I saw more fish and a huge whale,
It swam past, swaying its tail.

There were buildings everywhere,
And a clownfish that wanted to scare,
There was a cave quite far away,
Fish only go there in the day...

In the shark zone, sharks are having fun
Swimming around, playing in the sun
Moving everywhere as happy as can be
Proud little sharks beneath the sea.

Ethan Williams (10)
High Street Primary School, Barry

Underwater Land Poem

I dove down deep into the sea,
The fish dove and swam with me,
I gripped my torch in my hand
And shone it at an underwater land.

When I swam deeper into the ocean,
It was such a commotion,
There was a ton of motion,
Deep under the ocean.

When I dove from the boat,
I knew I wouldn't stay afloat,
I was in for a treat,
Away from the sun's heat.

When I looked up at the coast,
I saw some trees at most,
It looked like a barren land,
Compared to the underwater sand.

Vidor Anderung (10)
High Street Primary School, Barry

Underwater Land Poem

I dove down deep into the sea,
The fish dove and swam with me.
I gripped my torch in my hand,
And shone it at an underwater land.

Through the blue ocean,
I saw fish causing commotion.
As I swam under,
I started to wonder.

I saw coral and plants,
As I was in France.
I saw fish,
That were swish.

I saw a palace of wonder,
And right down under.
Were jewels of gold
That I then could hold.

I swooped through,
The ocean blue.

I swam down to flashing lights,
Down to taste some coral bites...

Sophie Edwards (10)
High Street Primary School, Barry

Underwater Land Poem

I dove down deep into the sea
The fish dove and swam with me,
I gripped my torch in my hand
And shone it at an underwater land.

I swam with the fish,
As they zoom and they swish
At the bottom of the ocean,
There is a lot of fast motion.

As the jellyfish sting,
The fish flap their fins,
As the submarines glow,
With the dolphins row by row.

When the hammerheads bite,
In the dead of night,
The fish try to escape
Their soon fishy fate...

Connor Ashill (10)
High Street Primary School, Barry

Imagination Land

I magination is my land
M agic all round
A dventures take you everywhere
G rape trees all the way
I n my land, chocolate-covered trees
N ow it's time to explore
A mazing magic getting stronger
T omorrow is another day
I mpossible to believe
O n top of the world
N othing stops imagination.

Sophie Dixon (8)
High Street Primary School, Barry

The Faraway City

Welcome to the city, far, far away
Everything is free
You don't pay
We have a fire station
It is very, very tall
The firemen are really cool
And look after us all
And the trees are sticky
They are made of chewing gum
If you'd like to pay a visit,
We would love you to come.

Joshua Perkins (8)
High Street Primary School, Barry

Candy Land

Candy Land is so, so sweet
Candy Land is bigger than your feet
The toffee trees are all around
The toffee trees don't make a sound
Everyone thinks that they are cool
Everyone loves the chocolate pool
The candyfloss is so, so yummy
I eat it up to fill my tummy!

Sara Osman (8)
High Street Primary School, Barry

Birthday Land

It's a happy land in Birthday Land
It is always sweet and bright
The children are so excited
They never sleep at night.

Beautiful presents all around
Decorated with bows.

Paper ripped and thrown on the ground
What's inside? Who knows.

Wendy Lian (8)
High Street Primary School, Barry

Unicorn Land

U nicorns are magical
N othing is impossible
I ncredible things happen here
C olourful hair and feathery wings
O n top of rainbows, unicorns dance
R ainbows shimmering over the land
N o one can believe their eyes.

Alexa Howells (7)
High Street Primary School, Barry

Mystical Creature

P owerful creature roaming around
H is feathers dazzle in the sun
O ut of the flames comes the phoenix
E legant wings to glide all around
N othing stops him
I t's magical
E X citing, deadly hunter, beware!

Griffin Enticott (7)
High Street Primary School, Barry

Gaming Land

In Gaming Land, I see children playing Fortnite and Minecraft
I hear gaming music and chatting
DanTDM is playing Roblox and Denis is too
I touch Xbox One controllers
I taste victory of winning!
I smell yummy chocolate cake for my pudding.

William Romans (7)
High Street Primary School, Barry

Emoji Land

E xcited emojis all around
M arvellous emojis, funny and exciting
O pen up your eyes and see emojis
J ust right for you
I t's Emoji Land, so come on down.

Savannah Abbott (8)
High Street Primary School, Barry

Rumble And Bumble

A volcano called Rumble
Who never grumbles
The one that mumbles
He is Rumble.

He is nice and big
He has a best friend
His name is Bumble
Who likes apple crumble.

Ciaran-Jon Curnick (10)
High Street Primary School, Barry

Candy

C andy Land is sweet
A nd amazing
N othing compares to Candy Land
D ads and mums like the place, Candy Land is like a dream
Y ou should go there.

Ellie May Stevens (10)
High Street Primary School, Barry

Food And Nightmare Land

F ood is in my land
O utside in the candy forest
O range sweets and candy canes grew
D own next to my land of nightmares.

William Llewellyn Jones (9)
High Street Primary School, Barry

Welcome To Candyland

Welcome to Candyland,
With lollipops and sweets to hand.
We have squirrels, dogs and cats,
Who have all grown rather fat.
Chocolate rivers with ice cream boats,
Sailing back and forth as they float.
We have popcorn fireworks,
Which make the people smirk.
There's a gingerbread castle on top of a hill,
With a king on a throne having a chill.
He has a crown made of gold,
To cover his bald.
He watches over his kingdom,
With so much wisdom.
Looking after his subjects,
With his pet T-rex.
The people feel grand,
Living here in Candyland.

Kenny Logan Risby (9)
Palmerston Primary School, Barry

Dig

It was a rainy day at my school.
Everyone was glum
Because they didn't know what was to come.

Into the classroom strolled a pig,
It was wearing a wig!
We told it to run,
"Run as fast as you can!"
But not as fast as the gingerbread man.

In came the teacher who taught us some more,
After the lesson we opened the door.
"Piggy, oh piggy, where did you hide?"
"Piggy, oh piggy, we are coming outside!"

We sprinted outside to find the pig,
Once we found it, we named it Dig.
We played and played with piggy all day.
This is a story that is here to stay.

Isabelle Woodward (9)
Palmerston Primary School, Barry

Candy Land

C andy canes are Christmas coloured.
A irHeads are very sour.
N erds are crunchy and colourful,
D ime is a famous chocolate bar.
Y orkie is milk chocolate.

L iquorice you can get in black and red.
A ero is minty and bubbly.
N estle Crunch is a crisped rice chocolate.
D olly mixture is different coloured sweets.

Casey Moores (8)
Palmerston Primary School, Barry

Park Life

One day I went to a park.
It was dark.
I kicked a ball over the wall.
So I gave my friend a call.
My friend brought a ball,
But we couldn't get over the wall.
Some weird-looking creatures
That had a big wig
And a slimy face
And no legs
Took the ball and played a little football themselves!

Gethin John Conway (9)
Palmerston Primary School, Barry

Guess Me!

I fly in the amber air,
I have rainbow hair,
I blow out glitter
But
I try not to litter!
I eat pink, delicious hay
And sing all day.

My friend Flower
has awesome powers,
Her wings are as soft as silk.
I have a pearl, colourful horn.
Who am I?

Lilly Lane (9)
Palmerston Primary School, Barry

Candy World

In through a portal,
I look and peek
At a beautiful candy world of sweets.

Slowly, carefully,
I feel my excitement
And I dig deeper, deeper, until...
I see a land of luscious sweets.

Yes! A lovely world at once!

Shelby Oliver (8)
Palmerston Primary School, Barry

Who Am I?

I fly in the bright blue sky.
I make magic through my horn.
I live in Candyland.
I like rainbows.
I like candy.
Who am I?

Skye Ford (9)
Palmerston Primary School, Barry

Wizarding World

Witches and wizards are everywhere
If you enter their world, you'd better beware
Fire-breathing dragons zipping through the sky
Trees so tall, I can hardly see that high.

A library full of spell books, waiting to be read
Wondrous potions running through my head
Big black cauldrons bursting with bubbles
Something lurking inside is going to cause many troubles.

Slimy, jumping toads the size of deer
Something all of the witches and wizards fear
Our eyes glisten, they're as big as the moon,
I wish I could fly there on my very own broom.

Beth Alicia Blank (11)
Pencoed Primary School, Pencoed

There Is Always A World To Decorate

My eyes slowly open,
The whole place is white
Until I rub my eyes
I don't think this is right!

My feet rose from the ground,
From two paper birds, majestic and bright
They begin to travel, wings flapping,
Now beginning to take flight!

I see coloured paint puddles all over the road,
And pens keep dancing along
This sky is yellow and pink and blue
My land has burst into song!

The trees are covered in bright tissue paper,
And cute paper animals hop in tune
Wooden people are walking, a smile on my face!
Singing whether sun or moon.

That water is made from baby-blue slime,
And kittens drink milk made from glue

But the thing is, quite daft if you think,
All day, the sheep go moo, moo, moo!

There is bunting round every corner,
Until my eyes meet a dull, empty place
People turn quiet and gather round!
What's this? One empty space!

As I scribble my name down in cursive,
We all begin to celebrate
And after this, I never thought I'd say…
But there's always a world to decorate!

Layla Stevens (11)
Pencoed Primary School, Pencoed

Dinosaur World

Imagine finding yourself in a world
Where dinosaurs were all around,
T-rexes crashed through giant rainforests
And pterosaurs swooped above the ground.

You would need to find a cave for safety,
Make tools to help you survive,
Learn to make fire from a simple spark
And hunt to keep alive.

Volcanoes would erupt and explode,
You would have to run for your life,
Trying to escape the lava flow
And fight anything with your knife.

Even plants could not be trusted,
Some could eat you too,
They would swallow you up and digest you
Into a disgusting kind of goo!

Oh no! A T-rex is on your tail,
You can only run so fast!

His jaws are just above your head!
Could this be your last...

Jack Anthony George (10)
Pencoed Primary School, Pencoed

Candy Kingdom

C hocolates and sweets galore
A nyone could dream of a kingdom like this
N o one could dread this magical place
D on't you just wish you lived here
Y ou can eat whatever candy you want.

K inder eggs, chocolate oranges and many, many more
I nside shops, all they sell is candy
N othing made out of wood or bricks
G uaranteed fun in Candy Kingdom
D on't need a holiday, just come here
O h, what a wonderful place to live
M mmm, lovely candy in Candy Kingdom.

Rhiannon Jade Witts (11)
Pencoed Primary School, Pencoed

Candy World

C ake is a number one dessert
A ero bars have two types of flavours: chocolate and mint
N utella is delicious on bread!
D airy Milk tastes smooth and silky
Y ou can never grow tired of eating candy.

W histle pops make you whistle
O reo is a black and white biscuit sandwich
R aspberry Maoam is so succulent
L ucien loves lollipops
D rumsticks are multicoloured candy on sticks.

Lucien Hope (7)
Pencoed Primary School, Pencoed

Football Crazy Land

F ootball is what I would play in my land
O n the lush green pitches, I will score lots of goals
O nce the whistle blows, I will run round and round
T housands of people having so much fun
"B rilliant," said the coach as I made a great pass
A ll of the players play really well
L oudly, the crowd cheer as the ball hits the net
L ots of fun we will have, playing football in my land!

Ieuan Taylor (8)
Pencoed Primary School, Pencoed

Candy Land

This land is tasty
Nobody is hasty
Trees and grass are made from cream,
This land of ours is such a dream,

The dragons here are our friends
The fun and laughter never ends
When it rains, the Smarties fall
When it stops, we eat them all.

To get around, we ride and fly
On the backs of unicorns in the sky
This land of ours is such a blast
It's the future, not the past.

Emrys James Curtis (8)
Pencoed Primary School, Pencoed

Sports Land

S wimming, ball games, athletics
P itches bright and green
O utside is the place to be
R acing to the finish line
T rack teams warming up
S occer, rugby, dodgeball.

L ong jump, gymnastics, hockey
A nd many more besides
N ever-ending motion
D o you think you would like to try?

Ethan Twine (10)
Pencoed Primary School, Pencoed

Football Fun

F ootball is fun
O utside, we get to run
O pposite teams we like to beat
T o score goals we need nifty feet
B eing in goal can be quite scary
A t half time, we start to feel quite weary
L ike Ronaldo it hits the back of the net
L et's do this girls, a few more goals, we haven't won just yet.

Eve Frayne (11)
Pencoed Primary School, Pencoed

Awesome World

A wesome World is a place to have tons of fun
W hen here in Awesome World
E xcitement and imagination is all you need
S low down, enjoy the rides and bright lights
O pen your mind, everything sparkles like we do
M eet new friends, be kind and laugh out loud
E njoy all we have to offer.

Fynnley David Farrow (8)
Pencoed Primary School, Pencoed

My Prehistoric Poem

D inosaurs are fierce and scary
I n Jurassic times they lived
N o longer do they exist
O ld dinosaur bones are called fossils
S ome dinosaurs roar really loud
A T-rex is a big meanie
U nderwater lives the ferocious monster
R un if you see a dinosaur!

Rhiannon Woodfin (8)
Pencoed Primary School, Pencoed

Origami World

O riginates from Japan
R eally tricky to do
I magine what it could be
G iraffes, pigs, elephants, they look so cool
A lot of patience is needed
M ake anything when you know the fold
I like Origami World but it's so hard to make.

Finn John Sewel (10)
Pencoed Primary School, Pencoed

Arts And Crafts Life

It feels like a wonderful dream
The grass is as soft as a puppy, it feels ever so sweet
It looks ever so dreamy it looks better than Disney!
It looks so delish you want to eat it
The shape is wonderful!
The shape is a pair of scissors cutting a piece of paper
It sounds like scissors are cutting paper!
It's so playful you can hear children's laughter
And birds singing
It sounds like a playful land
On one side it smells like beautiful fresh flowers
On the other side it smells like wonderful crafts
It smells like candy in a big giant corner
It smells so beautiful
You can eat it (it's worth eating).

Yaren Ince (8)
Severn Primary School, Canton

Magic Land

In Magic Land it looks like a big island that is a moustache,
In Magic Land it smells like bubbly ice cream,
Magic Land tastes like every food in the world mixed together,
Magic Land feels like the fluffiest cat ever
And sounds extremely quiet.

Isabel Drane (8)
Severn Primary School, Canton

Untitled

Arts and crafts looks like people doing arts and crafts.
Arts and crafts smells like paint
Arts and crafts tastes like paint air
Paintbrushes in arts and crafts feel like sheep wool.
Arts and crafts land.

Edward (7)
Severn Primary School, Canton

Monster Land

In Monster Land you can see electrons,
It smells like lizards in the sea.
It sounds like, *roar!*
It tastes like dinosaurs eating nuclear weapons.
It feels like fire!

Ali Butt (8)
Severn Primary School, Canton

Dark Land

Dark Land looks like puffs of smoke
Dark Land feels like hard cobblestones and rocks
Dark Land sounds like zombie voices
Dark Land tastes like flesh
Dark Land smells like burning fire.

Bailey Shay Williams (7)
Severn Primary School, Canton

Animal Land

In Animal Land it looks like 1,000 zoos stuck together.
It smells like pigs.
It tastes like chicken.
It feels like a sheep's fluff.
It sounds like birds chirping.

Millie Krebs-Jachimiak (7)
Severn Primary School, Canton

Hobby Land
(A Kennings poem)

Football-kicker
Football-maker
Punching-boxer
Fast-runner
Super-swimmer.

Taha Ibrahim (7)
Severn Primary School, Canton

The Land Of Dreams

In Dream Land,
You will see,
Wherever you go,
There will be...

Sparkling unicorns,
As our transport,
No cars allowed,
Not even in thought.

When you think of a bed,
All wooden and boring,
Well, we sleep in clouds,
And nobody's snoring.

You might think our pets,
Are a little bit odd,
Our dogs have very long ears
And our candy cane snakes
Sleep in giant pea pods.

No people in Dream Land,
As you might have guessed,

We have giant talking cookies
But I think the popcorn buckets are the best.

We have candyfloss trees,
And happy face flowers,
Talking mushrooms, no green vegetables,
Only in the disappearing towers.

So wonderful Dream Land,
It's the place to be,
As everything's here,
It's always happy.

Layla Gabica (10)
St Andrew's Primary School, Newport

The Darkest Light

Night-time can be so scary,
Especially when you think of Bloody Mary
Ghosts? Spiders? Spirits? That's what you hear
Until you realise it was all unreal
Terror dances around in your head
There's a voice saying, "Boo!" when you're in bed
Everywhere I go, someone will tap me and nobody's there
It always gives me a very big scare
Everything in my nightmare is scaring me
Horror is all I ever see!

Kayley Haynes (11)
St Andrew's Primary School, Newport

Candy World

In Candy World,
It rains a load
With delicious candy corn.

The peppermint man
Loves to have a good tan
And his peppermint dog
Loves to scratch on his log.

The candy cane queen
Loves her bean
And with her king, they sing.

There is a vanilla sea
Where the fish have their tea
There is a chocolate river
Where the snakes like to slither.

Sarah Curticean (11)
St Andrew's Primary School, Newport

Hamster Land

In a land of hamsters,
Who thought they were gangsters,
All lovely and sweet
With big orange teeth.

With a big squeaky wheel,
All others do is squeal,
Wood shaving floor,
And bars for a door.

Lovely and safe,
In our own little place,
Come and play,
You'll want to stay...

Shakyah Powell (10)
St Andrew's Primary School, Newport

Festival Of The Dead

The darkness twirls through the land,
Here they come, the skeleton band.
The spirits howl across the towns,
In ragged suits and shredded gowns.
From the mist, these zombies walk,
They jive and groove and talk the talk!
This deadly ball infects the skies,
With rotten flesh and even flies.
And when it's time for food, bugs are on the menu,
And rotten juice is what they drink at this vicious venue.
The music comes from beating drums,
They sing from mouths with bleeding gums.
This party made from skin and bones,
Swords will clang like sticks and stones.
They end the night in their graves,
And zombies sleep back in their caves.
Watch where you are going, you may just have a fall,
But broken bones are all the rage at the Skeleton Ball.

Khadiza Ali (11)
St Helen's Primary School, Swansea

The Enchanted Forest

The Enchanted Forest is full of magic and mystery,
It tells a tale from our darkest history.
About how the dark consumed the light,
And how a hero stood up to fight.
With long raven hair, and sea-blue eyes,
Her golden skin shone like the skies.

On the other side of the forest stood a malicious wizard,
Who held within his staff a blizzard,
Blood-red eyes and rotten teeth, stalking through the wood
His army rose around him to fight the forces of good.

The battle raged around them, tearing up the sky,
Light and dark came face-to-face, some had come to die,
The hero's power began to glow, feeding off the trees
It sealed the wizard deep away, his soul fell to the breeze.

The woods grew large and tall and strong
The plants refilled the ground
The forest came alive with song
Animals burst with sound.

The creatures above and beyond, from below and high above
Filled the Enchanted Forest with harmony and love
They praised their queen forever long, grateful for her fight
The saviour of the forest, who saved the day from night.

Tahmina Uddin (10)
St Helen's Primary School, Swansea

Mystical And Magic Kingdom

In a place far away, where people have picnics and play,
Is an enchanted forest and there lies a kingdom!
There are human werewolves and human cats,
But no human rats.
Elves and fairies dancing around,
And they will never be found.
As well as that, there's unicorns, phoenixes and many more!
They are the guardians and they stop wars!
Happiness is pure,
So there's no need for any cures.
The fairies live in flowers
And elves live in giant tree towers
A rainbow road leading to a castle of magic,
Which is elegant and fantastic!
In the castle lives a beautiful queen
She was a gorgeous and graceful human fox, who is never mean!

But there are rumours that a devil with utmost power,
Is locked up in a dark tower!
Apart from that, the kingdom is colourful, so come and visit!

Akram Ali (10)
St Helen's Primary School, Swansea

Mystical Land

The starry sky shines above, a navy shade of blue,
A castle in the distance, is calling out to you.
Across a river of dancing waves, a boat ride you must take,
Climb the stairs to be sorted, there's a decision we must make.
Which house will you be in? The brave, the bold or rude?
No matter which, the banquet hall is full of gorgeous food.
Next, it's to the classrooms, filled with chalk and books.
And a scary-looking professor, giving evil looks.
Down beneath the sparkly school lies the darkest part,
The dungeons creak and drip and spit, with a troll who farts.
Out on the grass, we ride our brooms, soaring through the sky,
The whistle blows a mighty blast as we learn to fly.

Nafisha Parvin (11)
St Helen's Primary School, Swansea

Horror Castle

The castle is dark on a dreary night,
The place to go when you want a fright,
Spiders and cobwebs line the walls,
And spirits linger in the halls.
White and slow, the ghosts dance,
Just join in when you get the chance!
With big long claws, and bright green skin,
The witches cackle, the spell begins!
The creaking walls are rotten and old,
They don't keep out the bitter cold.
Skeletons tumble in the halls
People get scared and spook us all!
Dark shadows against the ceilings,
Tall, dark, creepy beings
Howling screams in the corridors,
Creaky, wooden doors.
Watch out, a ghost is about,
Get ready to scream and shout.

Saamira Karim (11)
St Helen's Primary School, Swansea

Under The Sea

Under the sea and far away,
Fish and mermaids like to play.
They dive and dash through the reef,
Chasing crabs underneath.
The coral sparkles like twisted gold,
Down in the depths, it's bitter cold.

A chest of treasure lies in wait,
The swordfish swim, sharp and straight.
Water ripples through the sea,
Blowing bubbles for all to see.

The mermaids twirl and rise and dip,
The shells all rustle, dance and skip.
The waves rise high above the tide,
The dolphins soar with utmost pride.
And at the bottom of the sea, the kingdom falls asleep,
And all the lobsters come alive, and limpits starts to creep.

Alisha Ali (10)
St Helen's Primary School, Swansea

Wonderland

The land is ruled by the Queen of Hearts,
Who gobbles all the strawberry tarts.
She's mad, she's loud and rather mean,
Obsessed with red, but never green.
Then one day, there came a girl,
With skin like milk and eyes like pearls.
Alice, she was, a tough young thing,
And trouble she was sure to bring.
She met some wacky people, all along the way.
They sang and danced all the day away.
There's Rabbit, Cheshire and Hatter who is mad,
The Dormouse and the White Queen who is sad.
they battle on the chessboard to save all of the land,
From evil and buffoonery, fighting hand to hand.

Amina Khatun (10)
St Helen's Primary School, Swansea

Football Land

Yo! Welcome to Football Land
It's where you run around on the ground
Cheering loud, bouncing up and down
My kit is sparkling clean
Living the dream, with my football team.
The grass is green, and great, and growing tall
I keep my eyes upon the ball.
The ref is running round and round
My team are bounding, curving and swerving.
The minutes tick down on the huge round clock
Lots of goals, lots of ahhhs
The crowds go wild, man and child
Winning cheers, the whistle blast
The ball in the net, nobody fret!
What a goal, like taking a stroll.

Ali Utub (10)
St Helen's Primary School, Swansea

Bubblegum Land

The lanes are made of sticky gum,
And every soul is never glum.
The bubblegum king rules the land,
Popping candy, ever so grand.
There's cherry, cola and mint too,
All the colours from red to blue.
With trees of cotton candy, the sherbet grainy beach,
Toffee apples grow on trees, just out of your reach.
Chocolate coins and sticks of rock, and jumping jelly beans,
Bright and sour too, the sweetest you have seen!
Sweets of sugar make the clouds,
And liquorice whips fill the crowds.
Blowing bubbles in our gum,
And every soul is never glum.

Sara Nour (10)
St Helen's Primary School, Swansea

Christmas Land

There's snow falling all around,
Crunchy footprints on the ground.
Sparkling lights fill the tree,
The magic of Christmas is meant to be.
The presents sit in ribbons and bows,
The party starts and everyone goes.
There's glitter falling like soft snow,
And food and drink, that we know.
Father Christmas shows his face,
Sharing love and joy and grace.
Elves will dance their jolly jig,
And I will eat just like a pig!
It's Christmas Land, here in town,
Love and laughter all around.

Saabira Karim (11)
St Helen's Primary School, Swansea

Candyland

The skies are pink and filled with floss,
The candy cane lanes sparkle with gloss.
The hills are made of caramel,
In gingerbread houses, the people dwell.
The choc-o-river flows through the town
The candy stairs go up and down.
Jelly baby children race down the street,
With liquorice shoes on their feet.
All different shades of pink and green,
The sweetest children you have ever seen.
The days begin with gum and sweets,
And end with lots of sugary treats.

Tanzina Begum (11)
St Helen's Primary School, Swansea

Candyland

C reamy caramel, spilling like a waterfall
A ero bubbles fill the sky, popping like clouds
N uts and fruit stuff the chocolate streets
D ig in pits of candyfloss
Y orkie bricks make the buildings
L ollipops line the road, flashing like flowers
A pple toffee houses make the village
N ougat school and Snickers cars race down the lanes
D olly mixture children make friends with jelly babies!

Elena Velichkova (10)
St Helen's Primary School, Swansea

Horror Land

In a town where darkness sleeps,
Ghosts and spirits begin to creep.
The ancient bell begins to ring,
The dead will march, rise and sing.
Be very careful where you tread,
You may just even lose your head.
Inside homes are flickering lights,
And ghosts float, giving frights.

The spirits slither about the town,
gliding through the gloom,
You have to watch your back
or you'll end up in a tomb.

Riya Rahman (10)
St Helen's Primary School, Swansea

The Magical Unicorn Land

One magical day
A unicorn came to play
He jumped and spun
And ate a bun
And fell asleep in the sun.

He woke up smiling
And winked at me
I knew that was a sign
To come fly with me!

We flew around the city
We flew towards the sun
We spun around the clouds
Way up high.

The unicorn city was buzzing
People were rushing
Lights were flashing
Unicorns were skipping.

My rainbow city was full of fun
Toys and unicorns playing as one

Candy trees filled with sweets
Ice cream parlour full of treats.

Unicorn City was fantastic
Nothing was made of plastic
Everything was fresh and bright
Making children dream nicely at night.

Leaving Unicorn City
I hugged my unicorn friend
I hate saying goodbye
As we both love to fly.

One magical day
A unicorn came to play
My day was the best ever
Because I spent it with my friend forever.

Megan Rhys Godfrey (9)
Ysgol Gynradd Gymraeg Caerffili, Caerphilly

Come Where There Is Magic

Come to my land of magic
And I'm sure you will find nothing tragic
Clean your house with a whoosh of your wand
But don't send your furniture to the pond.

When the people hear the town bells
They get out their wands and do their spells
You can make a wish upon a stone
And you could be a princess on a throne.

You need to shop for your clothes
Before the shop gets up and goes
In this town you can never be lazy
Because it's always so crazy
The town is all a glitter
I better post this on Twitter.

Sophie Jackson (9)
Ysgol Gynradd Gymraeg Caerffili, Caerphilly

Candy Island

On Candy Island, everything is delicious
With gummy bears and colourful sensations,
Streets paved with flavoursome creations,
And trees offering tasty temptations.

Rivers flowing with thick chocolate,
Pink boats that are ginormous,
Carrying sweets which are enormous,
And all kinds of treats to warm us.

Come and join us in this paradise,
Something for everyone so come take a bite,
Your taste buds we are sure to excite,
And you can sample the island delight.

Meleri Ann Godfrey (9)
Ysgol Gynradd Gymraeg Caerffili, Caerphilly

Food Fantasy

In Food Fantasy
Everything's edible,
It's all incredible,
Not a speck of cement.

There isn't one piece of slate,
But a whole meal on a plate,
There's a honey fall
And an ice cream sandwich wall.

Children are loud,
For candyfloss clouds,
Hailstoning bonbons,
Snowing popcorn.
Come to this place,

Where there's not an empty space...

Isabella Ewings (11)
Ysgol Gynradd Gymraeg Caerffili, Caerphilly

Candy Kingdom

In Candy Kingdom, everything's free,
Mint-flavoured grass and caramel slides that make you scream wheee!
Toffee trees and chewing gum flowers galore,
When someone eats some, all they want is more
Gingerbread houses and icing beds,
Even their clothes are made of sweets, no threads
Candy Kingdom is the place to be
Eat as much as you like, it's all free.

Alice Elizabeth Todd (10)
Ysgol Gynradd Gymraeg Caerffili, Caerphilly

Cat, Cat

In the dark, zombies can eat
So remember to land on your feet.
Cats are in the day,
But in the night, they scare creepers away.
Skeletons burn in sunlight,
But in the night, they're up for a fight.
Eye of Ender tells where the Ender dragon is,
It must be opened.

Heulwen Crimmins (9)
Ysgol Gynradd Gymraeg Caerffili, Caerphilly

My Scarlets Land

Close your eyes
Follow me
To my Scarlets Land
Let my words be your guide,
And take you on a magic ride.
I see Scarlets playing in their ruby-red home kit,
I hear happy fans shouting wildly their rugby anthem,
I smell smoky sticky hot dogs in the stand,
I touch the scaly slippery oval ball,
I taste fish, chips, beans and candy, *mmmm!*
Aren't we lucky, you and I?
Our words are not just phrases
But alarm clocks
Ringing loud and clear
Awaking our five senses.

Ioan Jones (8)
Ysgol Nantgaredig, Nantgaredig

My Magic Land

Close your eyes,
Follow me
To my Magic Land
Let my words be your guide
And take you on a magic ride.
I see fairies in pink blossom trees,
I hear my dog barking when her eyes are sparkling,
I smell candy, just like brandy,
I touch my hair, flick, I just don't care
I taste curry, whilst I fill my tummy!
Aren't we lucky, you and I?
Our words are not just phrases
But alarm clocks
Ringing loud and clear
Awaking our five senses.

Grace Hobbs Rees (7)
Ysgol Nantgaredig, Nantgaredig

My Volcano Land

Close your eyes,
Follow me
To my volcano land
Let my words be your guide
And take you on a magic ride.

I see fiery, triangle volcanoes,
I hear volcanoes rumbling like thunder,
I smell volcanoes bursting,
I touch cold volcanic lava,
I taste tickling, sour volcano sweets.

Aren't we lucky, you and I?
Our worlds are not just phrases
But alarm clocks,
Ringing loud and clear
Awaking our five senses.

Carys Thomas (7)
Ysgol Nantgaredig, Nantgaredig

My Crystal Land

Close your eyes
Follow me
To my Crystal Land
Let my words be your guide
And take you on a magical ride.
I see crystals shining in the sunny light,
I heard birds chirping me awake,
I smell beautiful flowers,
I touch the peaceful grass,
I taste melting, edible crystal.
Aren't we lucky, you and I?
Our words are not just phrases
But alarm clocks
Ringing loud and clear
Awaking our five senses.

Honor Kernahan (8)
Ysgol Nantgaredig, Nantgaredig

My Candy Forest

Close your eyes
Follow me
To my candy forest.
Let my words be your guide
And take you on a magic ride.
I see raindrops dropping,
I hear horses trotting,
I smell Mami's perfume welcoming,
I touch diamonds floating,
I taste honey and caramel dripping.
Aren't we lucky, you and I?
Our words are not just phrases
But alarm clocks
Ringing loud and clear
Awaking our five senses.

Nancie Gooding (7)
Ysgol Nantgaredig, Nantgaredig

My Candy Land

Close your eyes
Follow me
To my Candy Land
Let my words be your guide
And take you on a magic ride.
I see slinky milk chocolate fountains,
I hear high-pitched candy music,
I smell strawberry lollipops,
I touch magical unicorns,
I taste rich caramel.
Aren't we lucky, you and I?
Our words are not just phrases
But alarm clocks
Ringing loud and clear
Awaking our five senses.

Betsan Quick (8)
Ysgol Nantgaredig, Nantgaredig

The Pirate Ship

My pirate ship land
Is totally grand
A fun and cool place
Where many ships race.

The ship is so big
You don't have to dig
To get to my prize
Which is big in size.

I have a cabin
Where lots can happen
So come to my base
The wonderful place.

Eluned Meredith Morgan (10)
Ysgol Trewen, Beulah

Blocks!

B ack to building
L ots of fun
O bsidian is hard
C ome to build and have fun
K nives and sword you see often
S tay playing Minecraft.

Kelsey Carter (8)
Ysgol Trewen, Beulah

Sweet Treat

This magical place is full of animals that race
Chocolate ice cream is always in my dream
Fairies that love to eat berries
Magical forests full of trees and a fresh breeze
Little homes, warm and full of gnomes
Chocolate waterfall on a tall, sweet mountain
Leaves on the beautiful trees
Swaying gracefully to the ground
Lollies on bushes with all kinds of flavour
T-rex is roaring and talking

S our lollipops on the bushes
W hile pink, pretty fairies dance around the ponds
E nchanting people are magic with their wands
E verything is magical in this place
T ime to go to sleep now come back soon and you will be found.

Gwen Sandra Samantha Nichols-Long (11)
Ysgol Y Ddwylan, Newcastle Emlyn

Don't Wish For What You'll Regret

Once there was a girl called Rose,
Who wore only white and red.
She went to Ysgol Buchan Gwen,
To try and make some friends.

She'd already read story books,
Of enchanted worlds and lands.
And sometimes wondered to herself,
Why can't I be like them?

But then one day, she fell asleep,
And found herself transported.
To a land where they planted jelly beans,
And picked off lemon sorbets.

She looked at all the people there,
All dressed in candy clothes.
Ladies wearing candy wrappers,
And men with liquorice monocles.

But suddenly, there was a fizzing noise,
And specks of gummy rain.

As she looked up,
With her two brown eyes,
She saw a bonbon coming her way.

When she woke up with an ouchy head,
She wondered where she had gone to next.
But when she saw the sand and sea,
She realised that she was in Capri.

The place where they wear yellow shirts,
Pretty purple flowers and short green skirts.
They had some bangles reflecting off light,
And pet fireflies shining at night.
Different for a person,
With a taste of red and white.

She felt discombobulated,
For what she had calculated.
That there was a little kitten,
Who had gotten separated,
Who had also accumulated.

The parts to get home,
The kitten who knows.

The one who was chose,
Had the name of Ninja,
Who eats hydrangea.

But she was nowhere to be found,
As she was chased by a hound.
As for Rose, you see,
She had learned that she was somebody!

Lili Pocsai (10)
Ysgol Y Ddwylan, Newcastle Emlyn

The Story Of Bob

Bob lives in his village and looks after his hens,
He scampers around and loves building dens.
His father is king and fights in the war,
Bob thinks he's a hero, but they're always poor.

His village has an airport, where Steve and Johnny work.
This is where he goes, and likes to lurk.
He wants to fly planes, high in the sky,
But he has to wear a smart suit and tie.

Bob's all grown up and he works in Defence,
His father calls him thick, but means no offence.
Bob's a bit *twp* and shot down a plane,
He went home to his wife - a girl called Elaine.

Ianto Lloyd (9)
Ysgol Y Ddwylan, Newcastle Emlyn

Untitled

His name was Football
He liked sitting in the hall
He never had friends
All he had were pens.

Then one day
He had a play
He was so round
He had a frown.

He was unhappy
Because he wore a nappy
He didn't like sport
Or the airport.

He was very poor
And all he had was sore
Then he wanted to go home
And sleep on foam
He got on a boat
And stayed afloat.

He got there
And saw a fair
He rode a ghost train
And saw a plane.

Then he went in a sweet shop
And started to hop
There was a bed
And he realised it was a shed.

Nyle Berry (10)
Ysgol Y Ddwylan, Newcastle Emlyn

A Frosty Night

Who is Jack Frost? Does anyone know where he lives?
Where does he go? Can anyone tell me is he thin or is he fat?
Does he wear baggy trousers or a nice bowler hat?

Is he warm?
Is he cold?
Is he young?
Is he old?
Does he sleep in the day? Does he work in the night?
Is he dark and handsome? Is he shiny and bright?

Every night, before bedtime, my mother will say
Jump into bed, now Jack Frost is on his way
I lie still and listen, I hear nothing at all.

Is that Jack Frost's shadow dancing on my bedroom wall?
Is he warm?
Is he cold?

Is he young?
Is he old?

Liam Evans (10)
Ysgol Y Ddwylan, Newcastle Emlyn

Candy Land

Candy Land is very sweet,
You can come here for a treat,
You can catch a chocolate mouse,
Or stay in a gingerbread house
You may also find some pleasure
By looking for golden coin treasure
Gummy shamrocks in the grass
Candy sheep going past
Cotton candy clouds in the sky
And the biggest aeroplanes flying by
You can hug a gummy bear
As for sleep, you prefer
Go to sleep in a tasty bed
With your tummy full and well fed
And if you wake in the middle of the night
You can grab another tasty bite.

Eirinn Amy O'Neill (9)
Ysgol Y Ddwylan, Newcastle Emlyn

Candy City

In Candy City,
Your teeth will get gritty,
There's plenty to eat
If you like something sweet.

The cinema is made out of a giant jelly bean
And in the Parma Violets castle, lives the queen
If you go into the forest, you better say a prayer
As in the forest, lives a hairy brown bear.

When you walk through Love Heart Way,
Be careful the Refreshers don't blow you away
The trees are made of lollies
So when it's raining sugar, don't forget your brollies.

Daniel Hulston (8)
Ysgol Y Ddwylan, Newcastle Emlyn

Unicorn Beat

Unicorns are fluffy and also very puffy,
They like the snow so they can glow,
They like the sky so they can fly so high,
They love millions to become billions.

There's a melted cheese river,
The gummy bears can shiver,
Their horns are made out of chocolate,
Their beds are made out of cookies.

The trees are still green,
But they are filled with ice cream,
And there's a unicorn queen who lives in a bobbly jelly bean,
I hope you enjoy candy treats.

Lacey (10) & Madison Hands
Ysgol Y Ddwylan, Newcastle Emlyn

Candyland

Candyland, Candyland, you are so sweet
Oh so colourful, pretty and neat
Your trees and flowers look such a treat
Lovely to look at and lovely to eat.

Candyland, Candyland, you are so nice
Lots of flavours, sugar and spice
Orange and strawberry, coconut ice
Lemon and lime and chocolate rice.

Candyland, Candyland, I wish I could stay
But now it is time that I must go away
I really enjoyed your grand display
And I will make sure I come back one day.

Evie Haf Denton (8)
Ysgol Y Ddwylan, Newcastle Emlyn

Dance Life

D ance is one of the things I like to do
A nd you can try it too
N ice turns in the air
C areful not to flick your hair
E ndeavour to point your toes, amazing costumes and pretty bows

L ively jumps across the floor
I nterpreting the space in front of the door
F ulfilling my needs
E ncouraging girls with their long hair and beads

Come on, give dancing a go
Graceful like a swan as you flow.

Halle Mai Evans (10)
Ysgol Y Ddwylan, Newcastle Emlyn

My Candy Shop

In my candy shop,
You can buy a lollipop
You can also buy some chewing gum,
Just be sure to hide it from Mum.

On the shelves are bags of toffee,
Underneath a machine that makes coffee
Into my shop, came Robert and Jane,
They both left my shop with a candy cane.

Too many sweets will make your teeth rotten,
Apples are healthier or had you forgotten?
Even when you're in a big rush -
Don't forget to use your toothbrush.

Alis Bevan (8)
Ysgol Y Ddwylan, Newcastle Emlyn

Dog World

Dog World is my favourite place
Where they run, jump and chat,
They love to lick and chase,
No lions allowed, not even a cat.

My dogs love to play when it is sunny,
They love to play when it is wet,
They jump over things, it is very funny,
That's what makes them the very best pet.

They come in all shapes and sizes,
Tall, fat, skinny, thin and small,
They all love to win prizes,
That is why I love them all.

Jack Dentten (10)
Ysgol Y Ddwylan, Newcastle Emlyn

The Haunted Castle

My dark and cold castle,
There are monsters lurking around,
It's silent and foggy outside,
And in the windows are eyes.

It's grey and there are shadows,
You don't think it's a monster, do you?
There is growling in the distance
And there are graves around you.

It's colourless and bleak,
You hear slithering and snarling,
You hear monsters,
Then boo!

And you're dead.

Amelie Gardner (10)
Ysgol Y Ddwylan, Newcastle Emlyn

Fairy Land

F airy Land is the name of my land
A nimals like unicorns live in Fairy Land
I n Fairy Land, everything is magical, pretty and sparkly
R ed mushrooms are homes to fairies and elves
Y ellow stars light up the sky at night.

L ights on the fairies' wands light the way
A ll the fairies are friends
N o unicorn has not got a horn
D o you want to go to Fairy Land?

Olivia Thompson Brook (8)
Ysgol Y Ddwylan, Newcastle Emlyn

Super Pencil

S uper Pencil is fast!
U sually, you need to be careful
P erhaps the evil scissors will scare you
E nemies of Super Pencil: Evil Scissors
R un everybody, run!

P oisonous chocolate lava
E veryone is scared!
N ow Evil Scissors has got Mr Paper
C atch him Super Pencil
I will cut him if I can
L ots of silence, Super Pencil saved Mr Paper.

Lola Thomas (10)
Ysgol Y Ddwylan, Newcastle Emlyn

Mountain Land

M ountain Land is my land
O ut come the zombies
U nder the blocks, they're
N owhere to be seen
T hey hide in the mine
A nd they die when the sun comes out
I n the dead of night
N owhere to hide.

L and is made of candy
A t the end of the day
N ight becomes darker and darker
D on't be afraid, no zombies are around.

Rhys Geraint Ridley-Bloom (9)
Ysgol Y Ddwylan, Newcastle Emlyn

I Love Music

I walked through a door and I was in a magical land.

L istening to the music
O f all different sounds
V iolins playing
E ating all different shapes and tastes.

M usic playing all around me
U nicorns are what I
S ee surrounding me
I smell all types as almost all instruments are scented
C ould you feel the funny feelings all around us?

Katie Ann Jones (10)
Ysgol Y Ddwylan, Newcastle Emlyn

Magical Candy Land

There was a magic land, far, far away
But not an ordinary magical land,
It was Magical Candy Land.
There was sugar as white as snow
Gummy snakes slither around eating the grass and mucking around
Marshmallow, fluffy beds
Children are made out of gingerbread
Trees made out of green gumdrops and pretzels
Candy cane lane
Unicorns are zooming through the sky and side to side
So come along and have some fun.

Lily Lamb (10)
Ysgol Y Ddwylan, Newcastle Emlyn

Sports Land

S ports Land is where I live
P laying rugby, football, cricket, darts and STS to name but a few
O ccasionally for a rest, it will be sports on the Xbox or the TV
R ugby and football I think are my favourite sports
T hirdly comes running, The Poppit 2K, running, running, running over golden sand
S ports Land is where I live, where we play and run and laugh together the whole day through.

Crwys Daniel (9)
Ysgol Y Ddwylan, Newcastle Emlyn

Newcastle Emlyn

Newcastle Emlyn is the name of our little village, which was situated in west Wales and was once said to be in Dyfed
The castle now is crumbling a little more each day and holds so many memories of times in the olden days
The river Teifi rages as it flows into the sea with walks around the riverbank for you and me to see
The market town is flourishing with shops that are unique so come along to see them and I think you will agree.

Tyler Dowling (8)
Ysgol Y Ddwylan, Newcastle Emlyn

My World Of Lego

L ego World is full of fun
E very day my world can change
G reat things happen when you build
O ver every hill you will find a new place.

W inding rivers flow through this land
O n top of mountains, dragons make their nests
R obot cows make Lego brick milk
L ego monkeys swing through the trees
D o you want to live in my Lego world?

Finley Stephens (9)
Ysgol Y Ddwylan, Newcastle Emlyn

Nightmares Land

N ight-time is dark
I try to stay awake
G hosts are creeping in my sleep
H aunting me
T rees are moving closer too
M ist is hanging in the air
A n eye is watching, I can see it there
R un, run, run before they catch me
E very step I go, they follow
S cream and I wake up in bed, Mum says it's okay, it's all in my head.

Callum Long (9)
Ysgol Y Ddwylan, Newcastle Emlyn

Animal Park

In my land of animals, there are lots of things to see,
You can even see an elephant climbing a tree,
Rabbits that bounce don't say very much,
They will either hop or munch, munch, munch
In my land of animals, there are lots of things to do
You can even see a hippopotamus sitting on the loo,
This is the place where animals love to play
Children can stay all day, hooray!

Amber Aryana Varrow (8)
Ysgol Y Ddwylan, Newcastle Emlyn

The Painter's Palette

In the painter's palette,
The sun is made of paint,
Sending out its colours,
So bright that you might faint.

Flowers grow like rainbows,
Every single hue,
Everything is bright and fresh
And always looks brand new.

There was a great painter
Whose art filled all this land,
But who didn't stay forever,
Now the brush is in our hand.

Loren Gwenllian Jones (8)
Ysgol Y Ddwylan, Newcastle Emlyn

Rainbows

R ainbows fall throughout the night
A rriving in Candy Land without a fright
I saw the beautiful rainbows in the sky
N oticeable colours shining bright
B lue shining brightest of them all
O h, how magical Candy Land can be
W ith rainbows and unicorns shining brightly, oh how great this place can be!

Katie Hunt (9)
Ysgol Y Ddwylan, Newcastle Emlyn

Skittle City

In Skittle City,
Everything's sweeties,
Not a speck of brick,
Not even a stick.

There isn't any grass,
Just a sticky toffee path,
It sticks like caramel,
And it tastes pretty good as well.

So get in your car,
It isn't very far,
Come visit this place
Where you can stuff your face.

Dafydd Nichols-Evans (9)
Ysgol Y Ddwylan, Newcastle Emlyn

Princess

Liase is as beautiful as a bunny
Donna's hair is dark blue and purple
Laa-Laa's crown is half red and half brown
My princesses are kind to people
My pink princess likes strawberries and blueberries
I love Laa-Laa's hair in the big blue sky on top of the world
I wish I was a pretty, lovely and kind princess.

Rafia Alam (7)
Ysgol Y Ddwylan, Newcastle Emlyn

Tetro Land

Gaming is the key in my land.
Playing here sure is grand.
Gaming to me is completing levels,
Gaming to me is defeating the devils.
Gaming is where Tetris blocks fall,
When gaming here, you'll have a ball.
Gaming with Pac-Man and Pokémon
All the way through Donkey Kong.

I love gaming!

Charlie Fillmore (9)
Ysgol Y Ddwylan, Newcastle Emlyn

Unicorn

U nicorns are amazing, they poo rainbow drops
N ever let the magic ever, ever stop
I ce cream is what they eat
C andy is my perfect treat
O ver the hill and far away, there lived a baby unicorn
R aining candy all over the land
N ot to fear, unicorns will always be here.

Layla Dowling (9)
Ysgol Y Ddwylan, Newcastle Emlyn

Jurassic City

In this city, there is a lot to see
And you will be shocked when you hear this treat,
You can stay for a while eating meat
The city is sometimes peaceful when the dinosaurs are sleeping
Or noisy when the dinosaurs are stampeding
So come and visit this place
So you will have a smile on your face.

Spencer Sando Varrow (8)
Ysgol Y Ddwylan, Newcastle Emlyn

Unicorn Land

U nicorn Land,
N ever give up on,
I cicles in Unicorn Land,
C olours everywhere,
O bviously, it's
R omantic and
N ever-ending.

L and everywhere
A nd unicorns
N ever stop eating and
D ancing.

Chloe Hatch (10)
Ysgol Y Ddwylan, Newcastle Emlyn

Candy Land

Yummy yum, it fills my tum,
Gummy bears, shake their spears.

Choco bridge, milky fridge,
Minty flower, candy power.

Icing roof, cotton candy proof,
Lemon dust, creamy crust.

If you come to join my fun,
Be aware of my creamy, dreamy, ginger man.

Julia Strzemkowska (10)
Ysgol Y Ddwylan, Newcastle Emlyn

World Of Football

Every day, I think about football.
I can taste the juicy hot dogs.
I can hear the loud singing, drowning the referee's whistle.
I can see the fans jumping in excitement.
I can smell the victory.
I can almost touch the Premier League.

Connor Dion Humphreys (9)
Ysgol Y Ddwylan, Newcastle Emlyn

A Demon Of A Dentist

There was a demon dentist
Who made the children cry,
She laughed and giggled to see
The children fear her golden eye
She made a magic potion
Fizz! Pop! Bang!
It made the children scared
And away they ran!

Mia Fulstow (10)
Ysgol Y Ddwylan, Newcastle Emlyn

Easter

E aster bunny is my favourite
A nd they don't stop hopping
S now is the colour of her coat
T iny Easter eggs hiding in the bush
E at all the eggs
R ound the family garden.

Sara Davies (8)
Ysgol Y Ddwylan, Newcastle Emlyn

Candy Land

C andy Land is a lovely place
A nd you might want a try
N ibbling on the jelly river
D unking biscuits in milk
Y ou will love the taste.

Marley Bussey (8)
Ysgol Y Ddwylan, Newcastle Emlyn

Balls

B ouncing, bouncing, loved by all
A s you hit against the wall
L isten to the drone
"L eave my windows be,"
S houts Mam to me.

Iestyn Kedward-Jones (10)
Ysgol Y Ddwylan, Newcastle Emlyn

Food

F ood is delicious
O h and it rots your teeth
O h, come to the palace, it is so fun
D ear dear, you get your hair stuck in the dessert side trees.

Ivy Thomas (8)
Ysgol Y Ddwylan, Newcastle Emlyn

Candy Land

Candy Land is fun
Sticky white chocolate everywhere
I eat it all the time
They are lush and sweet
You have the sparkle on your teeth.

Scarlett Poppy James (8)
Ysgol Y Ddwylan, Newcastle Emlyn

The Land Of Books!

The houses are shaped like little books
They have their own fabulous looks
The beautiful book birds flap their pages
For absolutely ages and ages.

The book trees sway from left to right
Watch out for dinosaurs, they will give you a fright
Rivers are fierce, fast and flowing
The big bright sun is always glowing.

On top of the hills is where I like to be
Reading author after author and feeling free
Clouds all around me, fluffy and white
All my favourite books together, what a wonderful sight!

No hustle or bustle of people passing by
Just me in my book world, glaring up at the sky
Come with me and visit my magical land
All you need is your favourite book in your hand.

Lainie Curtis (10)
Ystruth Primary School, East Pentwyn

Candy Kingdom

Welcome to my candy land,
All the other foods are banned,
Gummy bears are all around,
Sherbet sours are floating off the ground.

There's gingerbread houses with gingerbread men,
Creme eggs are laid by a magical hen
There's a creamy chocolate lake
With a bridge made of cake.

By the side of the caramel river
The gummy snakes love to slither
In front of each house is a candy cane
The only transport is the cookie train.

In this land, candy grows on trees,
It attracts lemon-covered bumblebees,
At this wonderful place,
You can stuff your face.

I really love this land of candy and caramel goo,
And I'm pretty sure you will love it too.

Olivia May Martyn (10)
Ystruth Primary School, East Pentwyn

Coding Kingdom

Over here at Coding Kingdom,
The binary buildings are not real,
Even though you're able to feel,
All the food is made of pixels,
Also including blocky pretzels.

All the pets ate NPCs
Although they will hop up on your knees,
All you do is program and code,
You could make your own water mode.

Any resource is bound to be near,
Or you can code it right by here,
Thank you for visiting Coding Kingdom
Come back soon to code with your children.

Rhys John Selwood (10)
Ystruth Primary School, East Pentwyn

The Magical Land Of Sweets

In Candy Land,
Other foods are banned,
Best land you'll ever meet
Everything is super sweet.

There's chocolate cement,
In the walls, there's not one dent,
Come visit the land of sweets
Stuff your face with delicious treats.

There's gingerbread men with icing so sweet,
They are delicious from their head to their feet,
Be careful with what you eat,
But everything tastes lovely and sweet!

Mia Hoskins (11)
Ystruth Primary School, East Pentwyn

The Land Of Colour

In the land of colour,
Nothing is dull or grey,
The land is full of joy and hope,
All throughout the day.

There is nothing that's grey or black,
And we will not let brown come back.

The beautiful sea is red,
The weird sand is blue,
Both weird and wonderful things are waiting for you,

The sky is green,
The grass is blue,
I love this place,
And so will you.

Grace Tandy (10)
Ystruth Primary School, East Pentwyn

Magical Candy Land

In Candy Land,
There is a candy band,
Eat candy canes,
There are no road lanes.

Go to the sweet shop,
You'll get a lollipop
Ride that candy kart,
Then shop at Walmart.

There are no trees,
Or little green leaves
The grass isn't green
Instead, it's fluffy cream.

Come to this sugary place,
Where you can stuff your hungry face.

Leah James (11)
Ystruth Primary School, East Pentwyn

The Magical Land Of Candy!

In Candy Land,
Nothing tastes bland,
Everything's pretty,
In this big city!

There's no wood,
It wouldn't taste good,
Watch out for the gummy snakes
They might be hiding in the chocolate lakes.

Come visit the land of sweets,
You can eat all your favourite treats,
It's the best land you'll ever meet,
Everything is really sweet!

Jessica Ann Griffiths (11)
Ystruth Primary School, East Pentwyn

Colourful Candy Land

Every day, it's candy in my world.

I hear kids laughing and giggling
I see a chocolate tree filled with cream and it's beautiful
I smell bubblegum and peppermint
I taste chocolate and candy and it's colourful like a rainbow in the sky
I feel sticky sweets and soft candyfloss.

In this world, it's lots of candy, come and show and make it with Andy.

Troy Shaun Thomas (10)
Ystruth Primary School, East Pentwyn

Pills 'n' Potions

Pink, purple, popping pills
Take one a day to cure your ills
Be careful of potions, they'll take your emotions
Take a red, makes you angry
Take a blue, makes you frown
Always take green, they'll make you happy
Potions make commotion at the ocean
Fuzzy, wuzzy bears with their
Fuzzy, wuzzy hair.

Grace Gwillym (10)
Ystruth Primary School, East Pentwyn

Candy World

C andy World is great
A nd no wood or brick
N o one will be bad
D on't go through the chocolate lake
Y ou can stuff your face.

L ove your favourite sweets
A ll of them are here
N o sign of the sun
D on't you know it's great?

Jack Williams (11)
Ystruth Primary School, East Pentwyn

My Land Of Unicorns

Unicorns have candy horns,
In my world it's bright and sweet
You get on with everyone you meet,
People riding their unicorns full of joy,
And their unicorns take them to
Where they want to go,
They're nice because they never say no!
Come visit this land,
Where fun is never banned!

Tayah Foulkes (11)
Ystruth Primary School, East Pentwyn

Why Unicorns Make Me Happy!

Unicorns make me happy
They smell like cotton candy,
They taste like rainbow Skittles,
They look so cute and fluffy,
They sound like horses neighing in the summer,
They feel like fluffy clouds
And that's why I love unicorns and
That's what makes me proud!

Ruby-Mae Perkins (10)
Ystruth Primary School, East Pentwyn

Music Land

M usic is my land and yours too
U se the instruments to play a magical tune
S leeping under the musical notes
I go on a guitar-shaped boat
C ome to this land of music and you will never forget it, music is for everyone as long as you let it.

Logan Carter (10)
Ystruth Primary School, East Pentwyn

Candy Land

Candy, candy everywhere
You know that there is lots to spare
In Candy Land, there's always some chocolate
Sweets and bubblegum,
Also, there is lots of cake
That is easy to make
Coco Pops and candy drops
Come to the land that they call home.

Grace Norris (10)
Ystruth Primary School, East Pentwyn

YOUNG WRITERS INFORMATION

We hope you have enjoyed reading this book – and that you will continue to in the coming years.

If you're a young writer who enjoys reading and creative writing, or the parent of an enthusiastic poet or story writer, do visit our website www.youngwriters.co.uk. Here you will find free competitions, workshops and games, as well as recommended reads, a poetry glossary and our blog.

If you would like to order further copies of this book, or any of our other titles, then please give us a call or visit www.youngwriters.co.uk.

Young Writers
Remus House
Coltsfoot Drive
Peterborough
PE2 9BF
(01733) 890066
info@youngwriters.co.uk